The

INFI
SU

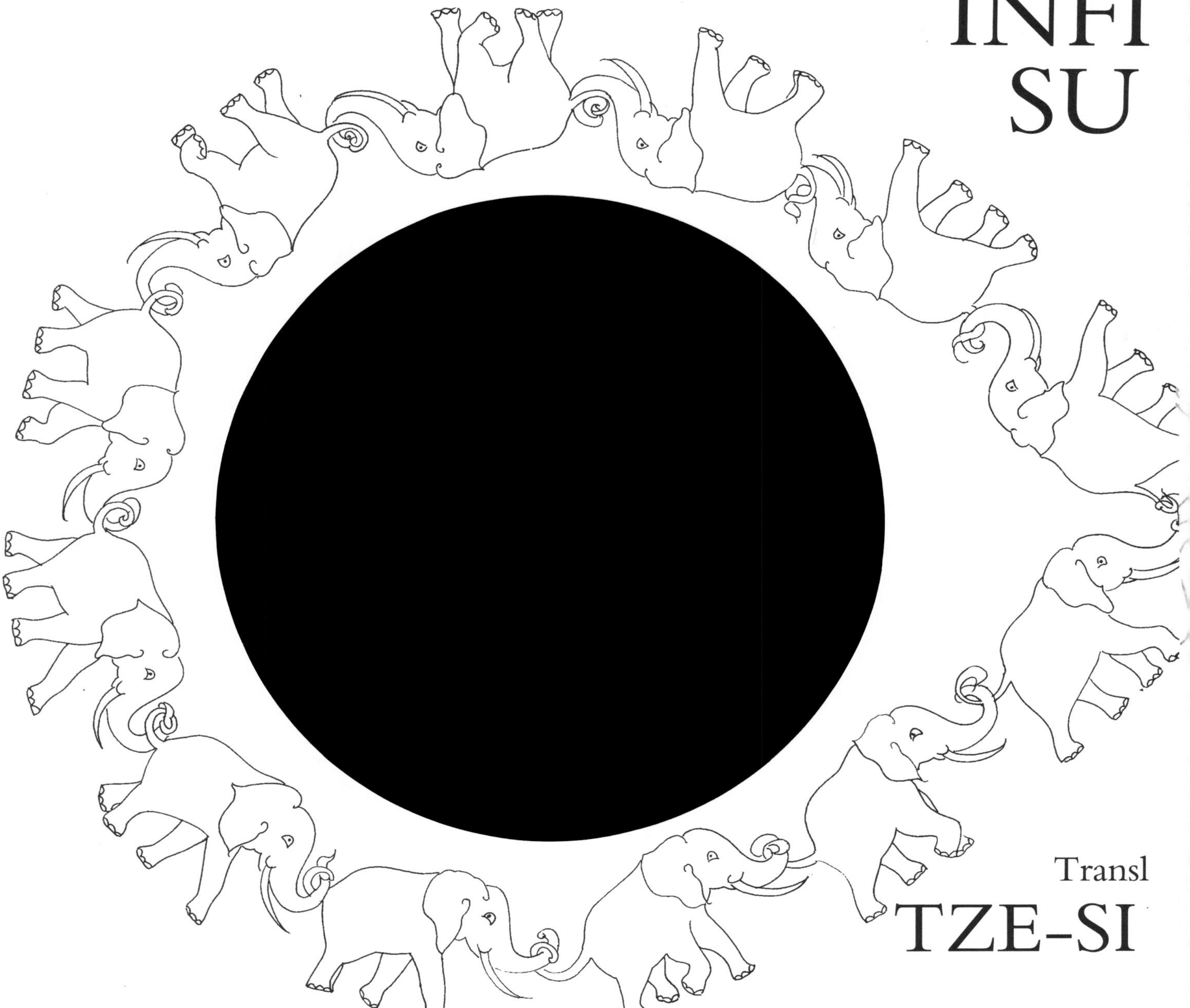

Transl
TZE-SI

Illustra
DE

NITY
TRA

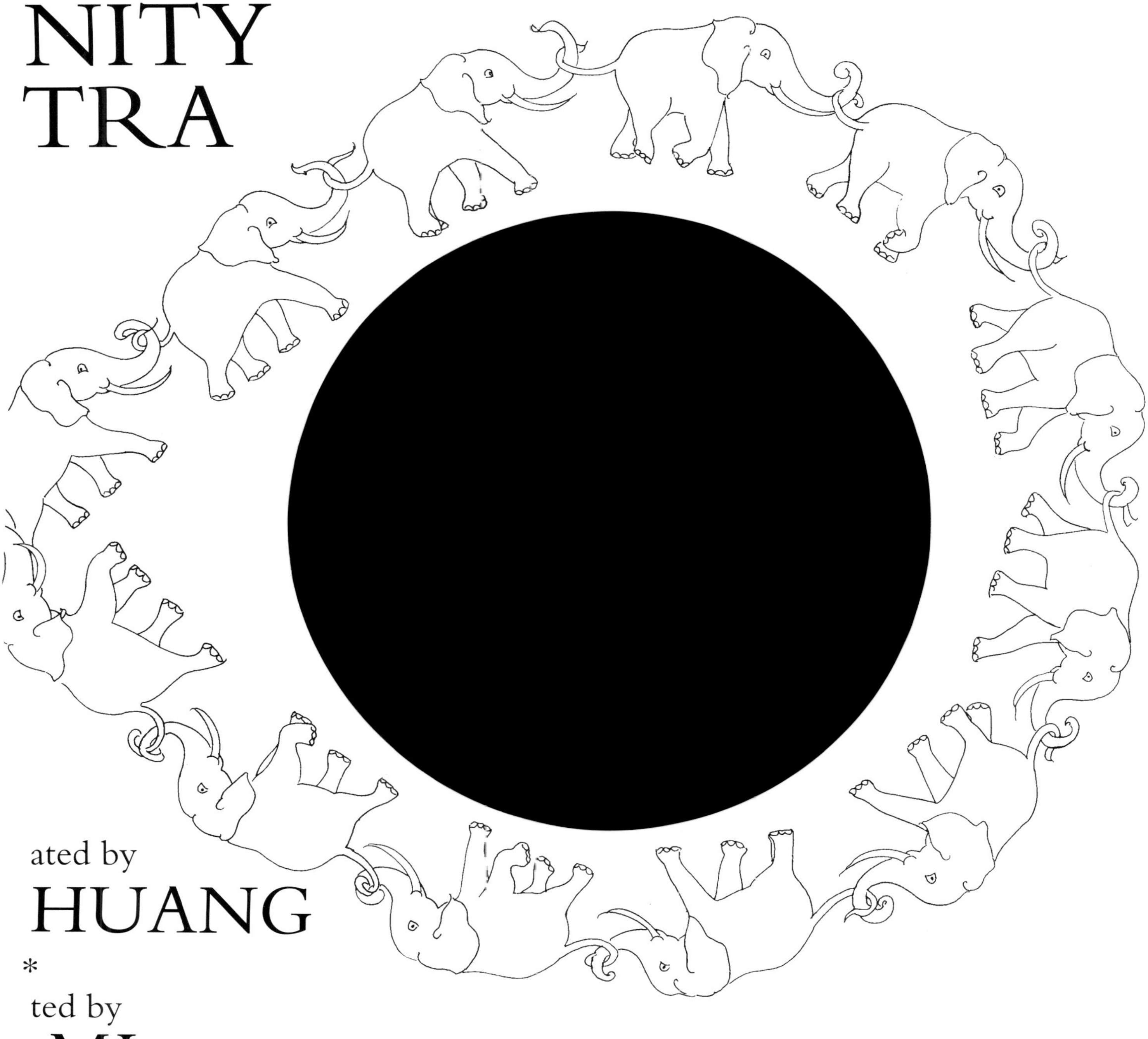

ated by
HUANG
*
ted by
MI

Buddha said to Udana,

nor water

nor fire

nor air,
for it is beyond the field of matter;

nor is it the sphere
of infinite space,

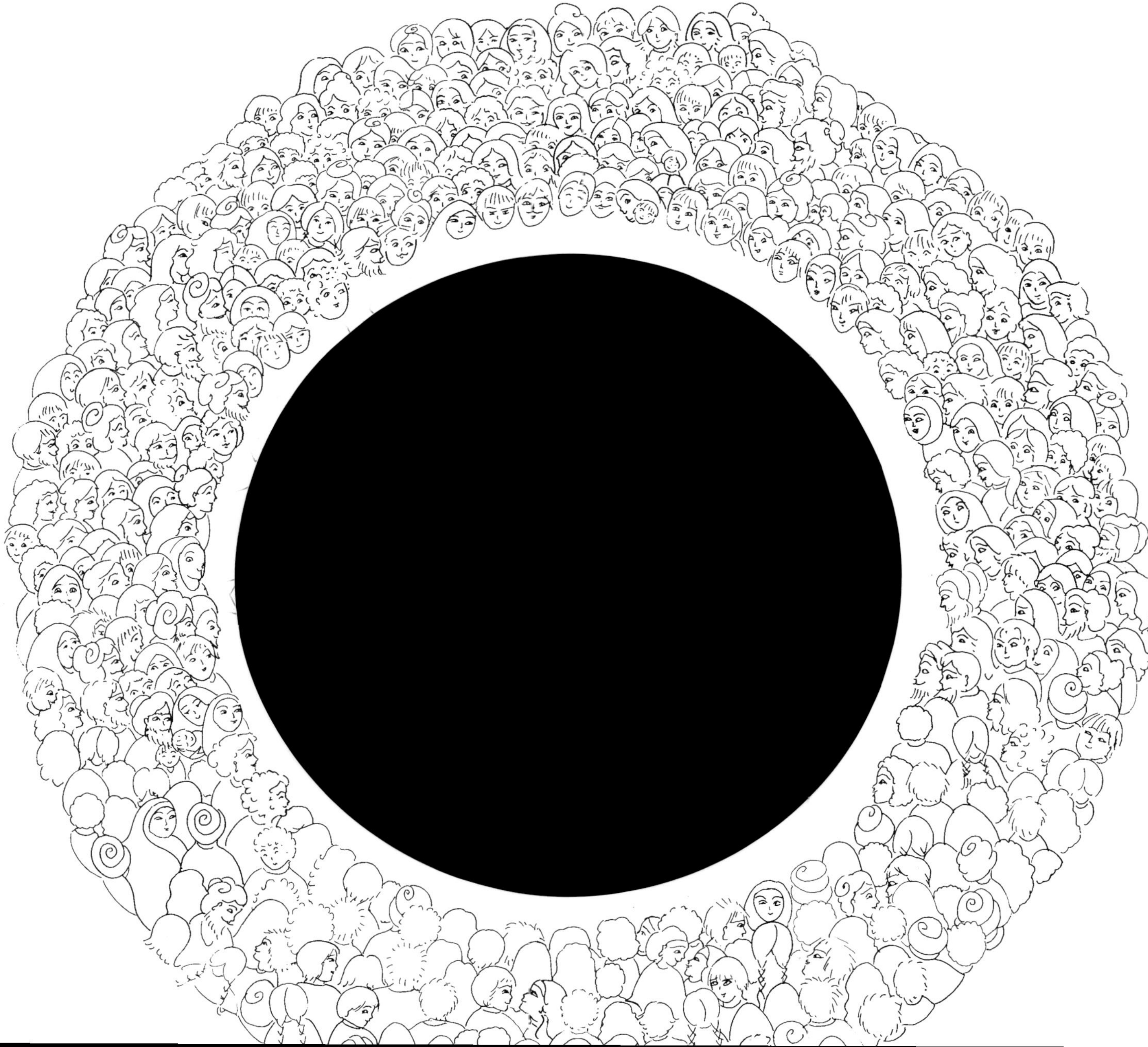

neither is there
the state of this world,
or another world,

nor sun

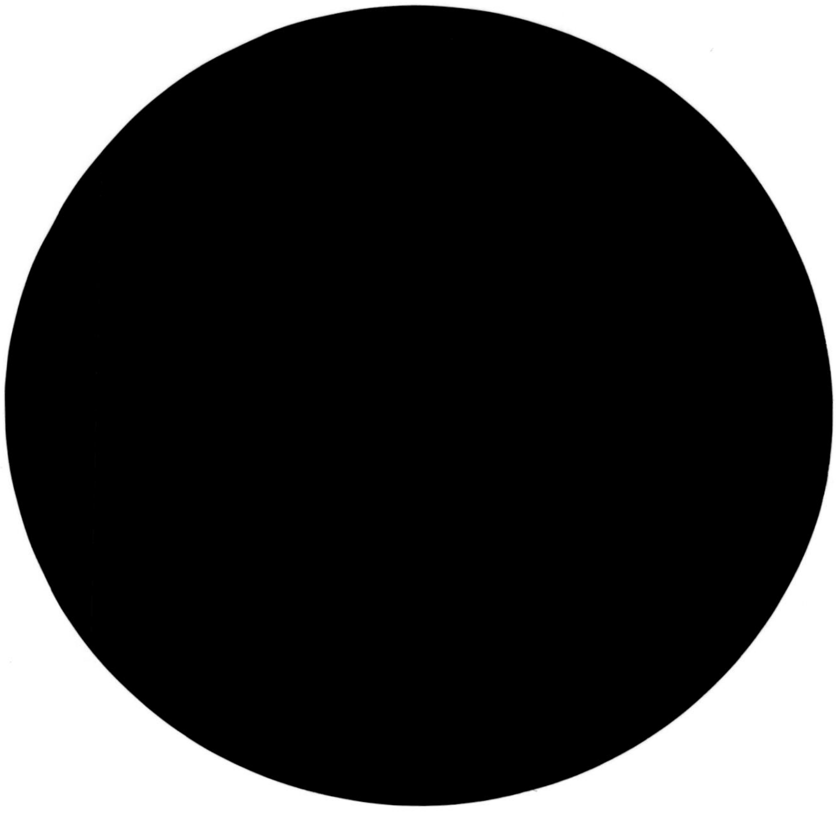

This is the

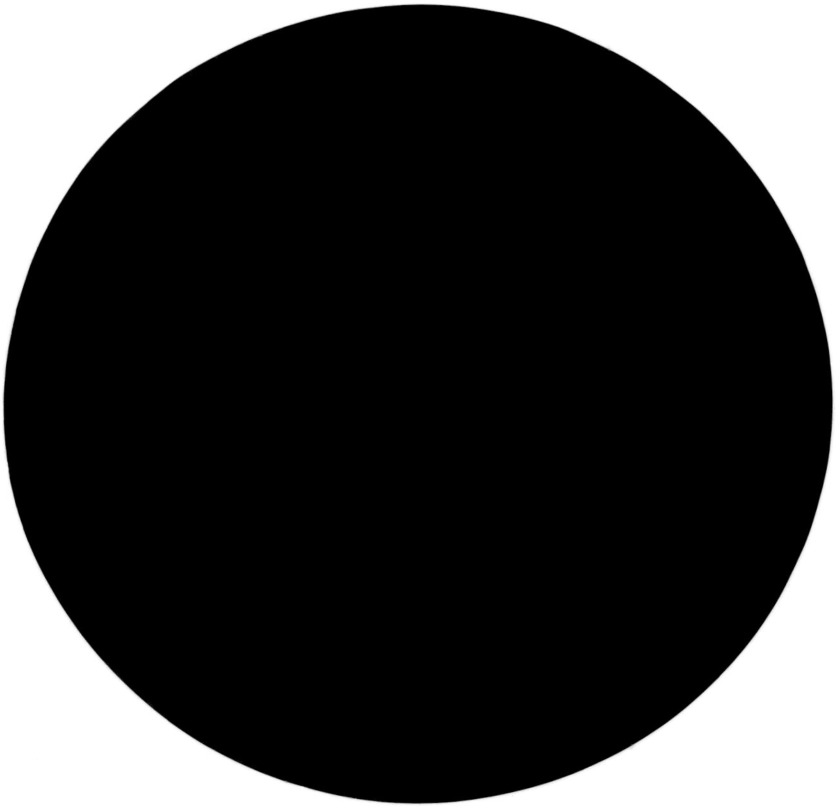

uncreated.

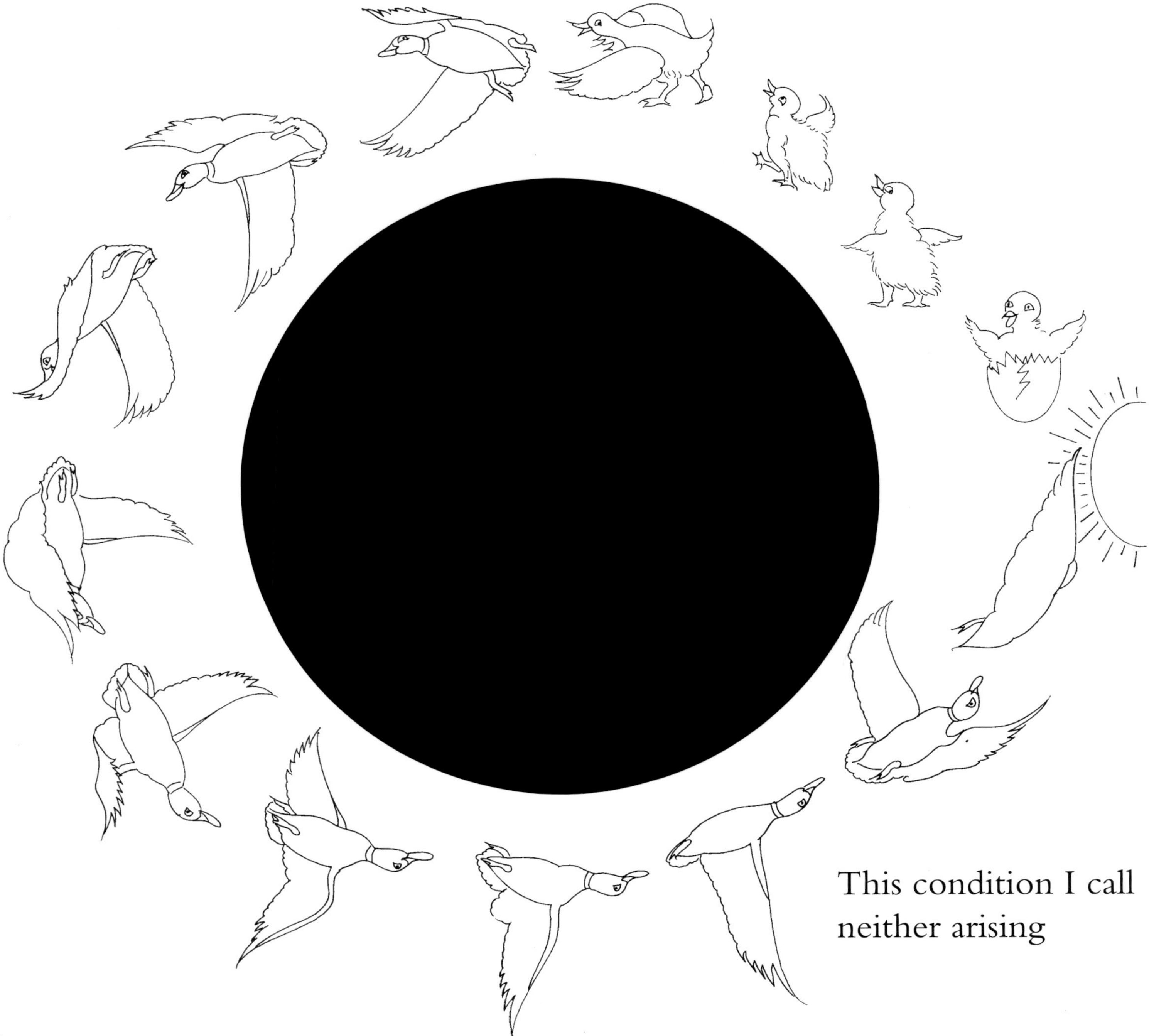

This condition I call
neither arising

nor passing away,

neither dying

nor being born.

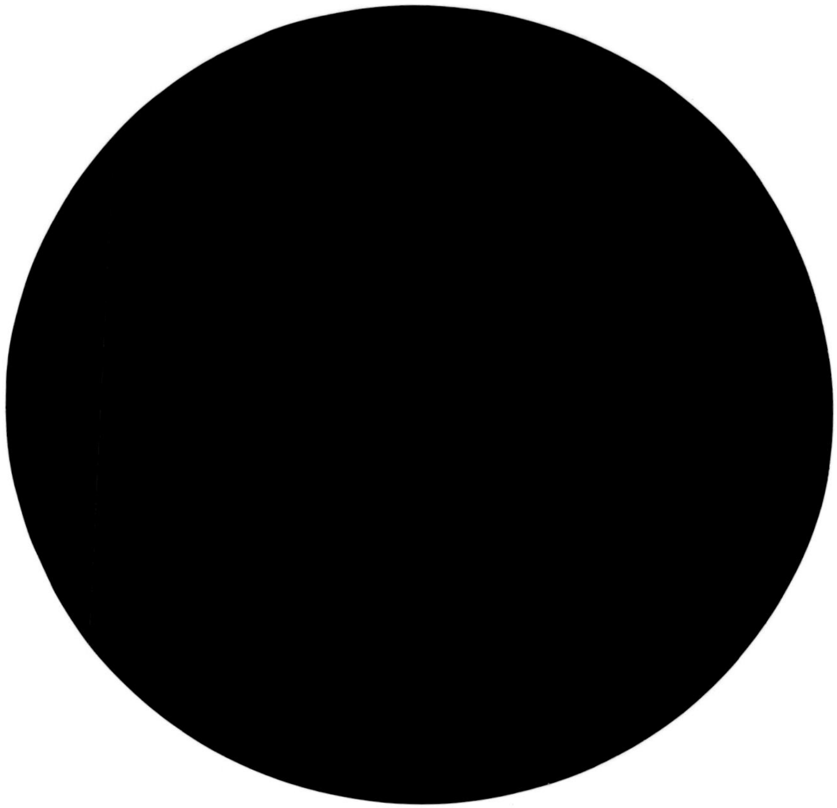

It is without form
and without change.
It is the eternal,
which never originates

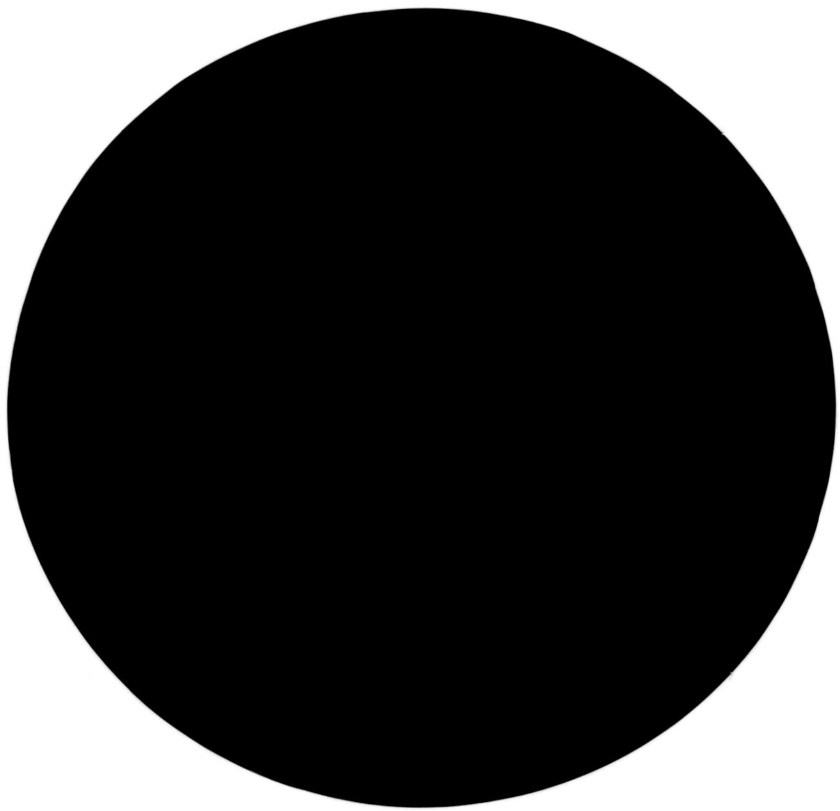

...and never passes away.
To find it
is the end of sorrow.

Buddha exclaimed,

"There IS this unborn,
uncreated, unformed,
and unconditioned.

Were there not this unborn, uncreated, unformed
and unconditioned,

there would be no transcendence from the world of the born, created, formed, and conditioned.

But since, monks,
there is the unborn,
uncreated, unformed,
unconditioned,

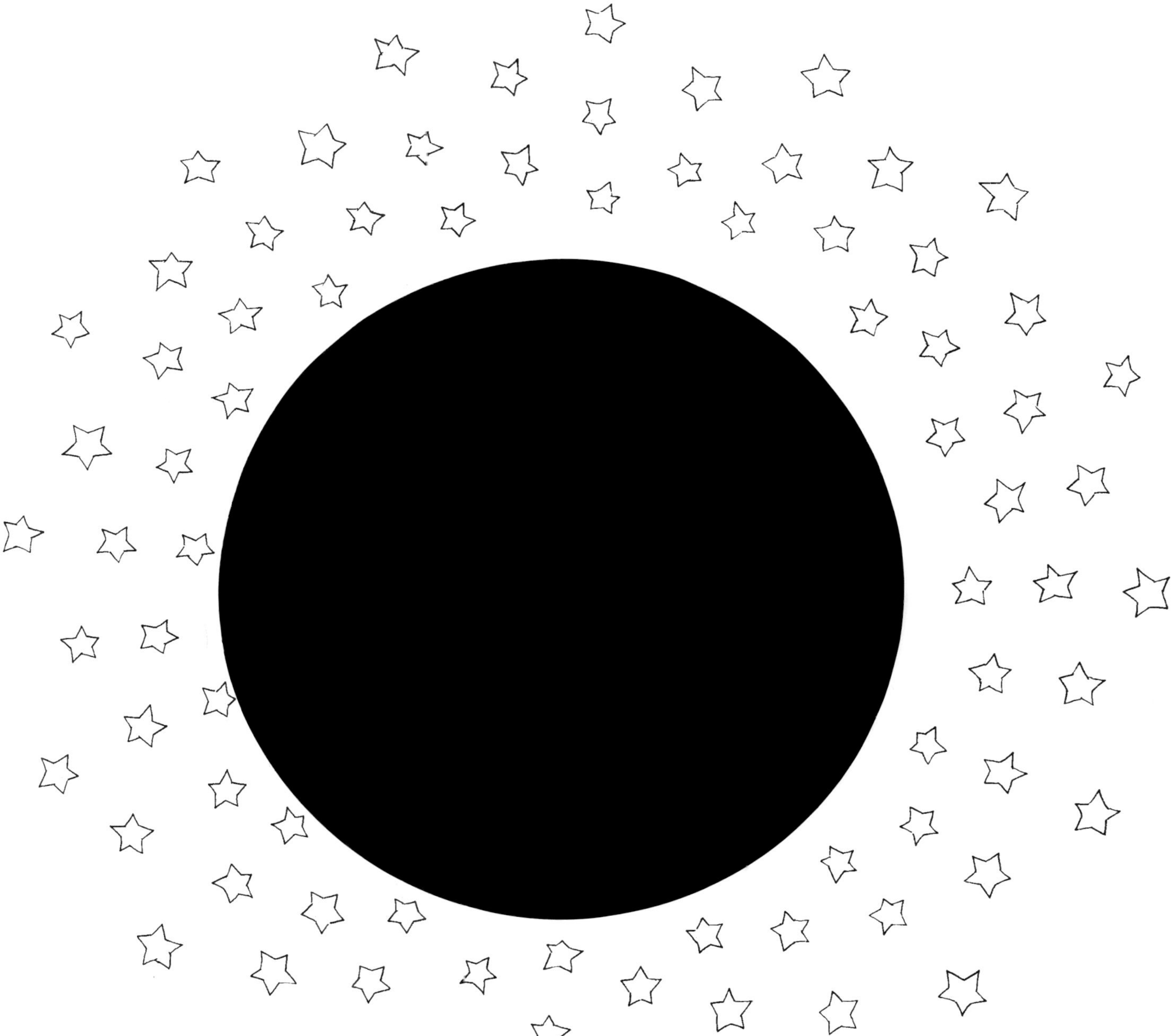

therefore there can be
transcendence for the born, created,
formed and conditioned!"

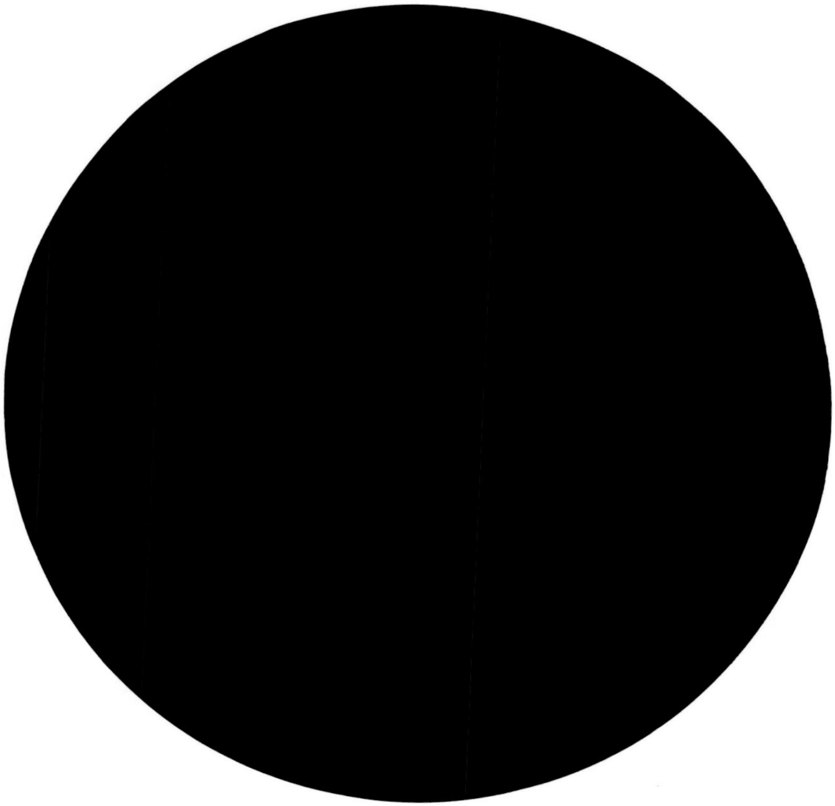

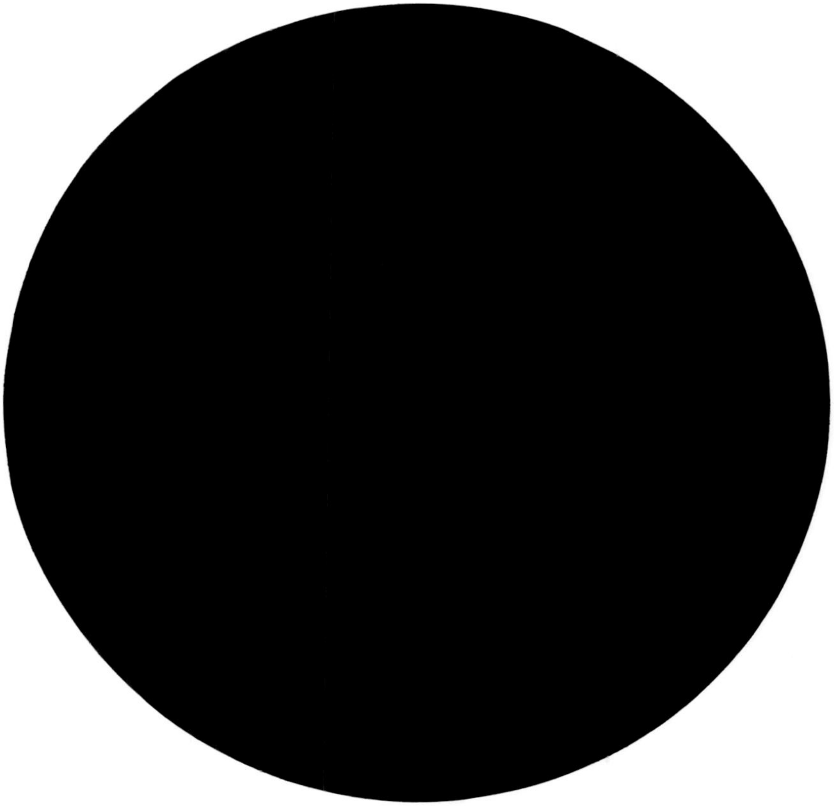

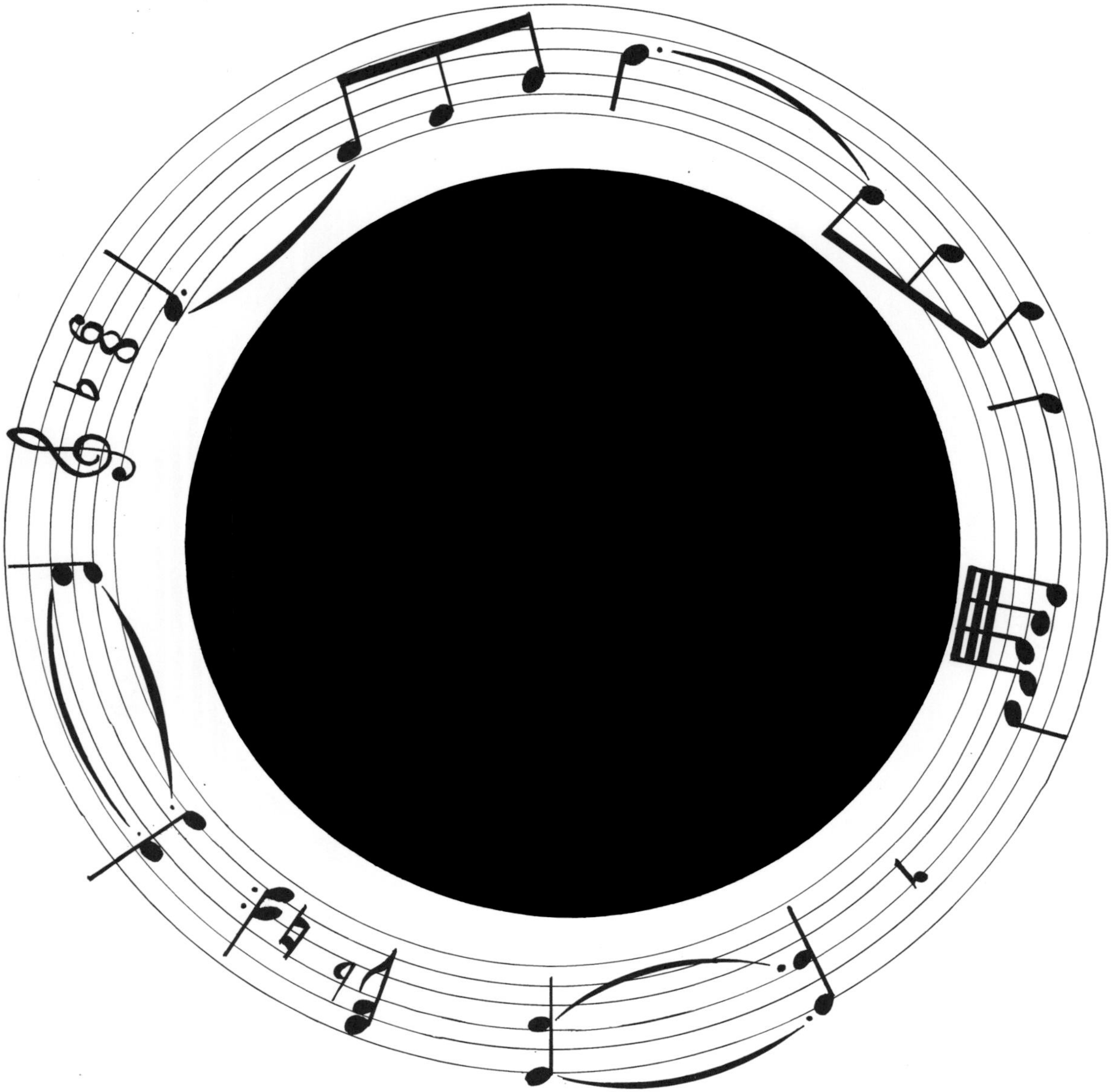

Honoring Eleanor

First published in 2024 by
Fons Vitae
49 Mockingbird Valley Drive
Louisville, KY 40207
http://www.fonsvitae.com
Email: fonsvitaeky@aol.com

ISBN 978-1941610-97-8
Library of Congress Control Number 2024931774
Printed in China